Alien

Adventures

Double Cross

Tony Bradman • Jonatronix

D1458349

Max's mission log

We are travelling through space on board the micro-ship Excelsa with our new friend, Eight.

We are trying to get home. Our only chance is to get to the Waythroo Wormhole – a space tunnel that should lead us back to our own galaxy. We don't have long. The wormhole is due to collapse very soon. If we don't get there in time, we'll be trapped in the Delta-Zimmer Galaxy forever!

To make matters worse, a space villain called Badlaw is following us in his Destroyer ship. Badlaw and his army of robotic Krools want to take over Earth. We can't let that happen!

Our new mission is simple: to shake off Badlaw and get to the Waythroo Wormhole before it collapses. I just wish it was as easy as it sounds.

Time until wormhole collapses: 4 days, 2 hours and 1 minute

In our last adventure ...

We flew into a time rift! Everyone on board was stuck in the rift except Cat and Tiger. They were outside the ship on a spacewalk when it happened so they weren't affected.

The Excelsa kept repeating the same five minutes over and over again. We needed one billion mega-whumps of energy to get free. However, the Excelsa did not have that kind of power.

Cat and Tiger teleported on to Badlaw's Destroyer ship. Together, they rewired his energy wrench. So when Badlaw fired it, instead of pulling us in towards the Destroyer, it pushed us out of the rift!

Chapter 1 – Damage report

"Hold on!" shouted Max, as another crackle of electric energy hit the ship. The Excelsa was in the middle of a major energy storm and was being tossed around like a cork at sea.

Max was worried. The storm was slowing them down. If they were going to reach the Waythroo Wormhole in time they couldn't afford any delays.

"The storm is affecting the controls," said Tiger. "I can hardly keep us on course."

"We'll be clear of it in a minute," said Eight.

Just then an alarm rang through the ship – WHOOP! WHOOP!

"**WARNING!**" said the ship's computer. "**Power surge!**"

Suddenly Cat's control panel exploded, BANG! BANG! BANG! Showers of sparks cascaded from it and the desk burst into flames.

Eight zoomed over with a fire extinguisher and put out the flames. The bridge was full of smoke and the acrid smell of burnt plastic.

The lightning outside the ship crackled and flashed, but it seemed to be moving away.

Soon, the storm faded completely.

"Thank goodness that's over!" exclaimed Max. "Ant, can you give us a damage report?"

"It's not as bad as it looks," said Ant, checking his screen. "A few circuits have blown in Cat's desk, which I can fix now, but that's about it. The rest of the ship seems to be OK too, although I'm getting a strange reading from the hold."

"It's probably nothing but I'll check it out, just in case," said Max.

In the hold was the fabricator, a machine that could make or copy anything. As Max approached, he saw a light blink on its control panel.

"*Umm, maybe a few of the lasers have blown,*" Max thought. He stepped inside the machine to investigate. Without warning, the door slid shut behind him and the fabricator started to hum.

Max tried to open the door but it wouldn't budge. He felt a funny, tingling sensation as rays of blue light scanned him. Then there was a *FLASH!* and a *ZAP!* Max fell to the floor.

After a few moments, Max slowly raised his head and saw ... himself. It was his double!

Chapter 2 – Mirror image

For an instant, Max thought he was dreaming. He shook his head, closed his eyes and opened them again, but the double was still there.

Max got to his feet and peered at his lookalike. He reached out and poked the double with his finger.

"Hey, who do you think you're prodding?" the double snapped.

Max jumped back, startled at the sound of his voice coming from someone else. The door to the fabricator slid open. He quickly stepped out, went over to a communi-screen, and called the bridge.

"Er, guys, could you come down here?" he said. "I think I need some help ..."

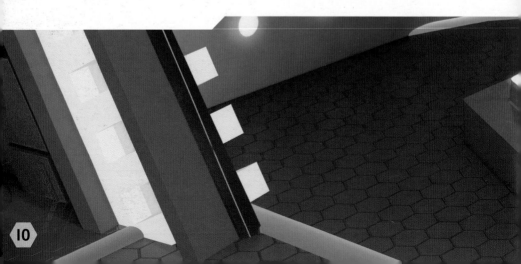

Tiger was busy steering the ship, so Cat, Ant and Eight went down to the hold. The sight of Max and his copy took them by surprise. Max explained what had happened.

"Oh no, that's all we need – *two* of you bossing us around!" said Cat, smiling.

"Ha, ha, very funny," said Max. "I don't like the idea of there being two of me either, Cat. The question is, what are we going to do with him?"

"You're not going to *do* anything with me," said the double. "I'm just like you, remember, so *I'll* decide what I do. Not you."

"I'd like to run a scan to see how alike you both are," said Eight.

"Good idea," said Max.

The double shrugged.

Eight took the double to the sick bay and the others followed.

The body scanner whirred and hummed as Max lay down. The scan didn't take long. Then it was the double's turn. Eight read the results from the screen.

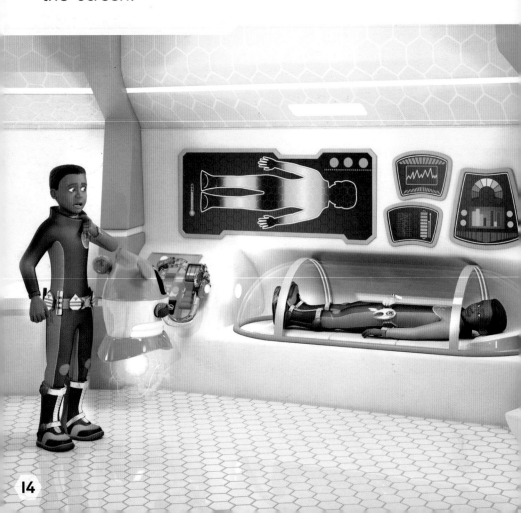

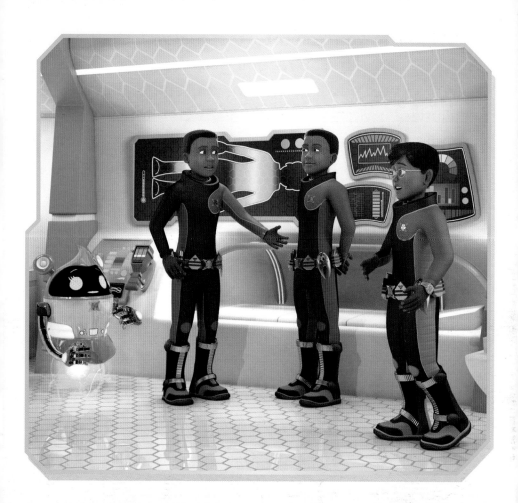

Eight turned to Max. "His body is exactly the same as yours," she said. "However, his brain pattern is different, so he may not think and act like you."

"Fascinating!" said Ant. "He looks the same as you, but he isn't you, Max."

"Er ... welcome aboard, Max Two," said Max, unsure.

The double just smirked.

"I suggest you come to the bridge," Eight said to Max Two. "If you're going to be part of the crew we will have to assign you some duties."

"Duties?" Max Two replied. "I don't like the sound of that."

"We all have to share the work," said Ant. "It's only fair."

Max's double went to the bridge with the others but he refused to do anything. He began messing around and making fun of Eight. Then he slipped away to play computer games.

"Eight was right. He doesn't act like you at all," said Cat to Max. "In fact, he's your *opposite*. You've always been a good leader, but he doesn't even want to join the team!"

Suddenly an alarm blared out from Cat's control panel.

"We're being scanned," she said. "That means there's another ship nearby." She checked her screen. "It's a long way behind us but it's catching up quickly. I should have it on the main viewscreen at any moment."

The crew held their breath as a familiar sight appeared on the screen – the dark shape of the Destroyer!

"Badlaw!" said Max. "Not again!" They were hoping that they'd got well away from the space villain, so they could reach Earth without him following.

"I'll try to shake him off," said Tiger. "Brace yourselves. It might be a bumpy ride!"

Chapter 3 – Badlaw's offer

Ant set the speed at level 6 and the Excelsa shot forward. Tiger tried all the fancy flying tricks he knew, but there was no escape from the Destroyer.

"What's Badlaw doing?" said Cat at last. "Why doesn't he just attack?"

"Hang on, there's an incoming signal," said Ant. "It's on the communication channel. Badlaw wants to talk to us."

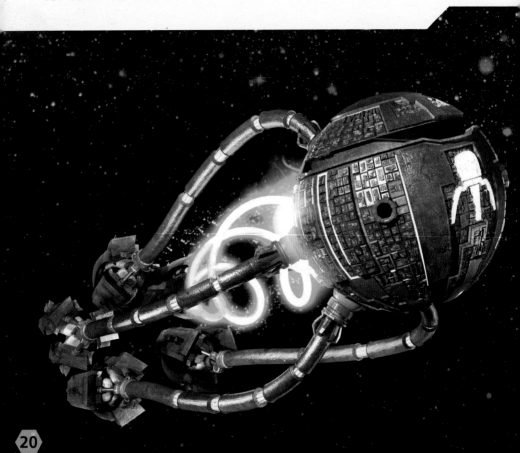

"I suppose we'd better talk to him," said Max, with a deep sigh.

Ant pressed a button on his control panel and Badlaw's face filled the viewscreen.

"What is it, Badlaw?" said Tiger. "We were hoping we'd never see you again."

"Ah, well you might just change your minds about that," said Badlaw. "At least, you might once you've heard my offer."

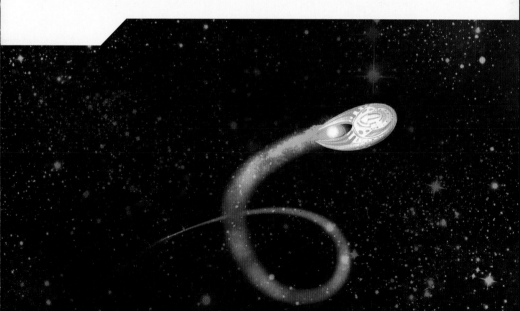

"We're not interested in anything you could offer us, Badlaw," said Max.

"Speak for yourself," said Max Two, who had come back on to the bridge and settled himself into Max's chair. "Let him tell us what it is first."

"Hey, be quiet!" said Max. "This has got nothing to do with you."

"Boys, boys!" said Badlaw. "There's no need to argue. My offer is very simple … I think we should work together."

"You have got to be joking!" said Tiger, utterly amazed.

"Oh no, I'm not," said Badlaw. "All you have to do is tell me where your home planet is and help me take it over. Then I'll make you joint rulers with me."

"Forget it!" said Cat. "That's the most ridiculous thing I've ever heard."

"I agree," said Tiger. "It would be a disaster if you took over Earth."

"It will be a disaster for you if I don't!" said Badlaw. "Obey me!"

"No," said Max, his face grim. "Cut him off, Ant."

Badlaw's face vanished and the screen faded to darkness.

"We've got to get as far away from Badlaw as we can," said Max. "Eight, is there any way we can outrun the Destroyer?"

"If we –" Eight began, but Max Two cut her off.

"I can't believe you lot!" he sneered. "We should accept Badlaw's offer!"

"How can you say that?" said Ant. "Badlaw is totally evil!"

"Can't you see how powerful he is?" said Max Two. "Look at his ship! It would be great to rule Earth. Just think about it ... no adults telling us what to do! We'd be totally in control!"

"We could never trust Badlaw," said Tiger. "So, no thanks."

Max looked sternly at his double. "You're out-voted. None of us wants to team up with that horrible alien."

The double shook his head, then stood up and went over to the door. "Suit yourselves," he said, and stomped off the bridge.

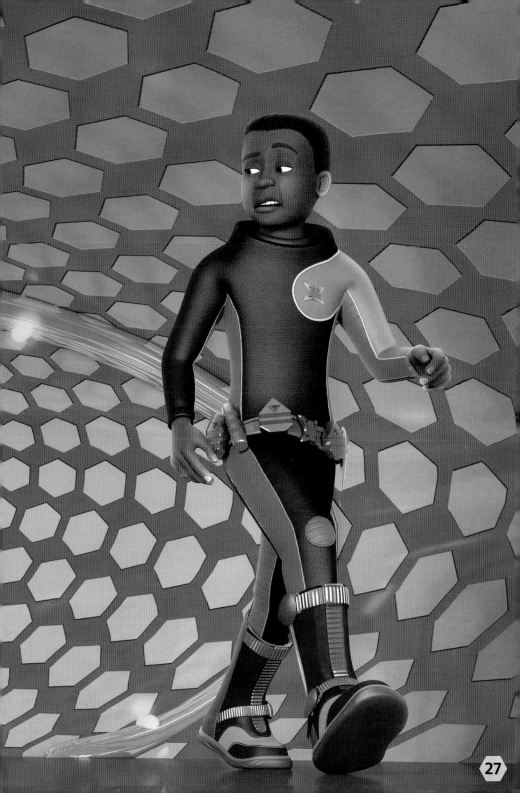

The doors of the bridge slid shut. Everyone went quiet.

Eight finally broke the silence. "As I began to say earlier, I have a suggestion for how we can get away from Badlaw. If we shut down as many systems as possible, we can divert more power to the engines. That should give us more speed."

"Sounds good to me," said Max.

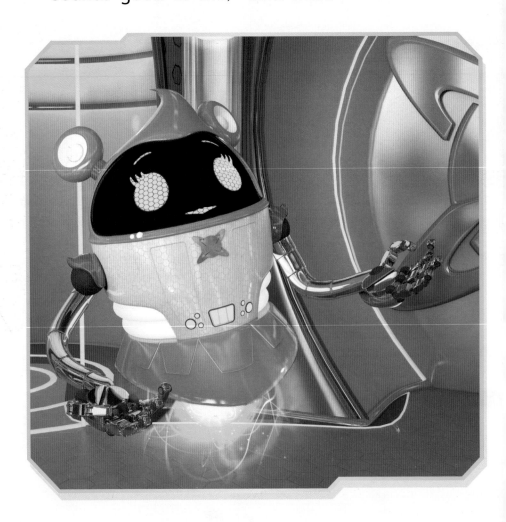

Ant immediately started shutting down systems they didn't need. Then he saw something on his control panel that made him frown. "I can't shut down the teleporter," he said. "It's not responding to instructions from the bridge for some reason. I'll have to do it manually."

Ant left the bridge and made his way to the teleport room. When he got there, he saw Max Two standing at the control panel. As soon as the double saw Ant, he ran to a teleport pad.

"Stop!" yelled Ant, but the double shimmered and vanished.

Ant ran to the controls to find out where he had gone. He thought Max Two might have put in the location of the nearest planet, but he hadn't. Ant checked the screen again and called the bridge.

"Max Two has gone!" he yelled into the communi-screen.

"What do you mean *gone*?" asked Max. "Gone where?"

"To the Destroyer!"

Ant hurried back to the bridge.

"Are you sure Max Two has gone to the Destroyer?" Max asked him.

"Yes, there's no doubt," said Ant.

"Well, good riddance," said Cat. "Badlaw is welcome to him."

"It could be a problem," said Eight. "Max Two knows everything you do, Max, including how to access the Excelsa's database."

"The location of Earth is in our database," said Ant, horrified. "That means Badlaw won't have to follow us any more. He'll be able to find Earth on his own!"

Suddenly every control panel on the bridge lit up and the screens started to flash the same message.

DATABASE DOWNLOAD: TWO MINUTES AND COUNTING ...

DATABASE
DOWNLOAD:
TWO MINUTES
AND COUNTING ...

"He didn't waste much time, did he?" said Tiger.

"Can you do anything to stop them, Eight?" asked Max quickly.

"I'm afraid not, Max," said Eight. "I can try to make the download process more difficult, but I cannot keep them out entirely."

"Do whatever you can," said Max. "At least it might give us time to think."

Eight tapped away at the controls. All the screens on the bridge flickered like crazy, but the same message kept flashing as before.

"So what are we going to do?" said Tiger. "Any suggestions?"

"Yes," said Cat. "We should let Badlaw have the database."

Everyone turned to stare at her, their mouths open in shock.

"What?" said Max.

"I don't mean let him have the *real* database. I mean we could make a copy of it with the wrong route to Earth," Cat said.

"Genius!" said Ant. "But is there time?"

"I think so," replied Eight. "I might also be able to hide something in the copy that will stop Badlaw in his tracks, too."

"Eight, Cat, get to work," Max said. "I'll try and distract Badlaw. Ant, contact the Destroyer and put Badlaw on the viewscreen."

Ant hurried back to his desk. Seconds later Badlaw's ugly face appeared once more. This time Max Two was standing beside him. Both of them were grinning.

"Er ... we've been thinking about your offer, Badlaw," said Max.

"Is that so?" said Badlaw. "Well, it's too late! Thanks to my new friend here, I don't need you any more."

"That's right, and despite your attempts to keep us out, we should have access to your database very soon," said Max Two.

Their images disappeared and another message flashed on the screen.

DATABASE DOWNLOAD: TEN SECONDS ...

Max looked over at Cat and Eight. "How are you two doing?"

"We need more time!" Cat shot back.

FIVE ... FOUR ... THREE ...

"Come on, guys," said Max. "We're depending on you!"

TWO ... ONE ...

"Done!" said Cat.

A loud humming noise started, and a new message appeared.

DATABASE DOWNLOAD: COMPLETE.

Badlaw reappeared on the screen. He began to gurgle with laughter. "Thank you for the database," he said.

"Yeah, thanks!" said Max Two, with a sneer. "See you on Earth!"

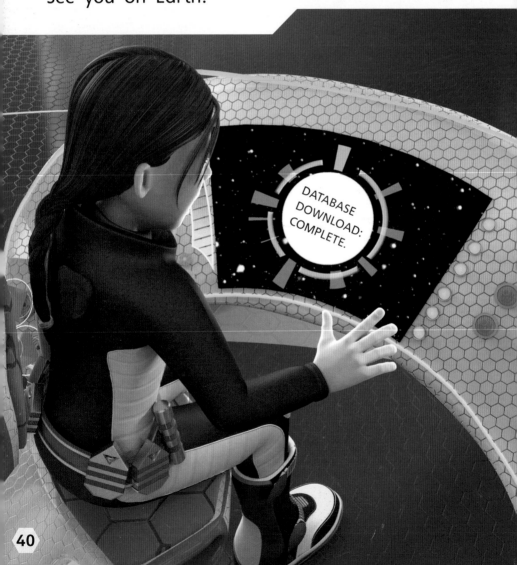

DATABASE DOWNLOAD: COMPLETE.

"Oh, I doubt you'll see them again,"
said Badlaw.

"What are you talking about, Badlaw?"
said Max.

"Now I have the route to Earth, I don't need
you any more. I can finally get rid of you! FIRE
ALL LASER CANONS!"

"No!" cried Max.

Chapter 5 – Explode code

A storm of energy balls flew through space, straight at the Excelsa. Alarms went off, lights flashed and everybody yelled.

"Quick, Tiger!" said Max.

"I'm already on it," Tiger said. He flung the ship into a downward spin, speeding past the sizzling energy balls.

Suddenly three Krool pods flew out of the Destroyer and zoomed towards the Excelsa.

"Hold tight!" cried Tiger. He looped the loop. The Krools tried to follow him, but they couldn't turn quickly enough. Their pods spun out of control, crashed into each other and exploded in a shower of metal.

Tiger barely had time to steady the ship before Ant cried, "Look at that!"

The Destroyer had come to a juddering halt. Flames and smoke poured out of its engines.

"What's happening to their ship?" asked Max, confused.

Eight smiled. "I added an explode code to the dummy database," she explained.

"An explode code?" asked Ant.

"Yes, it caused the Destroyer to malfunction."

"I don't think Badlaw will be bothering us for a while," laughed Tiger.

"We should still get as far away as possible," said Max. "Full speed ahead. We haven't got much time to get to the wormhole."

A couple of hours later, Eight found Max in the sick bay. He was looking through the scans of Max Two.

"What's going to happen to my double now?" he asked Eight. "Can we find a way to teleport him back?"

"He's too far out of range, I'm afraid. I do not think he will return to this ship," replied Eight.

Max shuddered. "I don't like the thought of him being out there in the universe," he said. "It's not easy knowing that there's someone who looks exactly like me, but acts in a way I never would."

"Then let us hope your paths never cross again," said Eight.

Unknown to the crew of the Excelsa, at that very moment a small craft zoomed out of the Destroyer. Inside it was Max Two.

"I'm not staying with Badlaw. He's far too bossy," he muttered, as the spacecraft soared into space. "And there's a great big universe to explore out there ..."

Find out what happens next in *The Rust Monster*.